MW01165064

Veggie - Fruit - Nut

MUFFIN RECIPES

by Darlene Funkhouser

HEARTS 'N TUMMIES COOKBOOK COMPANY
A Dinky Division of Quixote Press

3544 Blakslee St.
Wever, IA 52658
800-571-2665

LIST OF RECIPES

SOME WORDS FROM THE HEART

Nothing says love and comfort more than a nice, warm muffin you baked _yourself_. There are "he-man" muffins, heart-smart muffins, and decadent dessert confections _so_ rich and luscious it's almost a sin to eat one... or two... The muffins in this cookbook are quick, easy-to-make crowd pleasers. No matter if you want a healthy muffin to launch you on your busy day, one to lovingly pack in lunches, or treats that will make you the absolute envy of get-togethers, the recipe is in this book.

Enjoy, God bless, and happy baking!

MUFFIN TINS

There are three basic types of tins:

1) Standard muffin tin – the "workhorse" of muffins, it makes twelve regular-sized muffins.

2) Texas muffin tin – makes six huge muffins; bake 5-10 minutes longer than standard muffins.

3) Miniature muffin tin – makes twenty-four small muffins; bake 5-10 minutes less than standard muffins.

BEFORE YOU BAKE

Preheating - Always preheat the oven for ten minutes. Preheating is essential for producing nicely-shaped muffins.

Greasing - To grease muffin cups:

1) Use vegetable cooking spray; or

2) Use paper or foil baking cups (no need to grease). If you use paper baking cups, let muffins cool completely or they might stick to the paper when you pull it off. If you like hot or warm muffins, it's better to use cooking spray.

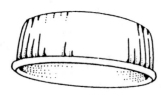

Flour – All recipes in this book use all-purpose flour unless otherwise noted; always stir flour before using it, because it settles in the bag. Stirring allows air to get into the flour (it lightens flour up) and ensures that you will not get too much in your muffins.

MORE BEFORE YOU BAKE

Coconut – Use shredded coconut (canned or bagged).

Roasting nuts: Some people like to roast nuts before adding them to a recipe, others prefer them raw. Roasting is simple: Spread nuts on a baking sheet in a single layer. Toast in a preheated 250o oven until they reach the desired brownness (45-60 minutes). Don't overroast.

Filling muffin cups – I fill cups 3/4 full because I like large muffins. If you prefer smaller muffins, 2/3 full is better.

<u>Freezing</u> - Put muffins in a zip-lock bag; cool muffins completely before freezing.

<u>Reheating</u> - Place muffin in a microwave for 30-50 seconds, or in a conventional oven at 300o for 10 minutes.

SUBSTITUTIONS

Buttermilk - Don't run out and buy buttermilk!
You can "make" your own by adding 1 tbs lemon
juice or 1 tbs vinegar to 1 cup of milk. Let set
for five minutes before adding to ingredients.

Cake flour - If you don't have cake flour, use 2 tbs
less of all-purpose flour per cup.

LOWFAT TRICKS

<u>Any</u> of these recipes can be made lowfat by:

1) Using skim milk rather than whole
2) Using margarine instead of butter
3) Using whites rather than whole eggs:
     2 whites = 1 whole egg
4) Using unsweetened applesauce to replace oil (fat) in a recipe. Use 3/4 applesauce to

replace all of the oil:

 example: 3/4 C applesauce to 1 C oil

If mixture seems too dry, you may need to replace
all of the oil with an equal amount of applesauce.

Note: Lowfat muffins bake quicker than regular
ones; a toothpick test is needed sooner.

APPLE

1 egg, beaten	3/4 C milk
1 med apple (chopped)	2 C flour
1/2 C vegetable oil	1/2 tsp cinnamon
3 tsp baking powder	1/4 tsp nutmeg
1/4 C sugar	1/2 tsp salt

Combine egg, milk, oil. Add remaining ingredients, mix into a lumpy batter. Fill 12 greased muffin cups 3/4 full, bake at 400o for 20-25 minutes.

APPLE BRAN
(Low Fat)

3/4 C whole wheat flour
½ tbs baking powder
2 egg whites
1/2 C bran
1/4 tsp baking soda
2 tbs oil

1 tsp cinnamon
1/4 C raisins
1 tbs molasses
1 apple, chopped
1/3 C milk

Combine first five ingredients; add apple. In
another bowl, mix remaining ingredients. Stir wet
ingredients into dry. Fill 6-9 greased muffin tins
2/3 full, bake 20-22 minutes at 400o.

APPLE CHEDDAR

These muffins are like hot apple pie topped with cheddar cheese.

1½ C flour	1½ tbs sugar
2½ tsp baking powder	1/2 tsp salt
1 egg, beaten	3/4 C milk
1/3 C vegetable oil	1/4 tsp allspice
1/2 C shredded cheddar cheese	
1/3 C quick-cook rolled oats	
3/4 C finely chopped apple	

Combine dry ingredients and apples; make a well in center. In another bowl, mix egg, milk, oil. Pour into well, stir to a lumpy batter. Fill 12 greased tins 3/4 full and bake at 400o for 18-20 minutes.

APPLE-NUT STREUSEL

1 egg, beaten
1/2 C vegetable oil
1 med apple, chopped
1/2 tsp cinnamon
3 tsp baking powder

3/4 C milk
2 C flour
1/2 tsp salt
1/3 C brown sugar

Streusel topping: 1/4 C brown sugar, 1/4 C chopped
nuts, 1/2 tsp cinnamon

Combine egg, milk, oil, apple. Add remaining
ingredients (except topping), mix into a moist,
lumpy batter. Fill 12 greased muffin cups 3/4
full. Top with streusel, bake at 400o 25 minutes.

APPLESAUCE

1 egg	2 tsp oil

1½ C unsweetened applesauce
3/4 tsp baking soda
2 tsp baking powder

¼ tsp nutmeg	½ tsp cinnamon
½ C raisins	½ C ch walnuts

2 C flour

Mix first three ingredients;
add others. Fill 12 greased
tins 3/4; 375o 25 minutes.

APPLESAUCE MAPLE
(Can be sugar-free)

2 C pastry flour   1 tsp baking powder
1/2 C maple syrup*   1/4 tsp cinnamon
1/4 tsp allspice   1 egg
1/2 C raisins   1/2 C chopped walnuts
1¼ C unsweetened applesauce
*Diabetics can use sugar-free maple syrup

Combine flour and baking powder, stir well. Add wet
items, stir to moisten; fold in raisins and nuts.
Fill 12 greased cups 3/4 full; 350o 18-22 minutes.

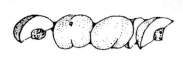

APRICOT

2¾ C flour	1 tsp baking soda
1/4 tsp cinnamon	2 tsp baking powder
3 eggs, beaten	1½ C sugar
1/2 C vegetable oil	1 C buttermilk
1½ lb dried apricots (cooked and mashed)	

Combine flour, baking soda, cinnamon, baking powder.
Mix in another bowl eggs, sugar, oil. Add flour and
buttermilk alternately, add apricots. Fill 8-10
greased tins 3/4 full; bake at 350º 25-30 minutes.

BACKPACKER

These loaded-with-health, tasty muffins will satisfy
the hikers, campers, and outdoorsmen in your family.

1½ C whole wheat flour	2 tsp baking powder
1/2 tsp salt	3/4 C rolled oats
1 C skim milk	1 egg
3 tbs butter, melted	2 tbs molasses
1/2 tsp cinnamon	1/2 C raisins
1 C sunflower seeds	1/2 C chopped walnuts
1 12 oz package semi-sweet chocolate morsels	

Sift together flour, baking powder, salt. Add oats,
raisins, chips, seeds and nuts. In another bowl,
mix wet ingredients. Combine mixtures. Fill 12
greased cups 3/4 full; 400o for 20-25 minutes.

BACON-CHEESE

2 C flour
2½ tsp baking powder
1 C buttermilk
1 egg, beaten
1 C diced, crisp bacon

1/4 C sugar
1/4 tsp salt
6 tsp butter, melted
1 C shredded cheddar cheese

Mix dry ingredients; stir in wet items, mix well.
Fill 12 greased cups 2/3 full, 400o for 20 minutes.

BANANA

1 egg, beaten
1/3 C milk
½ C vegetable oil
2 C flour
¼ C brown sugar
1/4 tsp salt
1/2 tsp cinnamon
½ C chopped walnuts (opt)
3 tsp baking powder
1 C mashed banana
Mix egg, milk, oil. Add
other items, make a lumpy
batter. Fill 12 greased
cups 3/4, 400o 25 minutes.

BANANA BLUEBERRY
(Sugar-free)

2/3 C mashed banana (mash with fork)
1 egg   1/2 C milk
1/3 C vegetable oil   2 C unbleached flour
1 tsp baking soda   1 tsp baking powder
1 C blueberries fresh or frozen (thaw, pat dry)

Cream banana and egg; add milk and oil. Slowly add
flour, baking soda and powder, beat well; fold in
berries. Fill 12 greased cups 3/4; bake at 350o
for 15 minutes (lightly browned).

BANANA FIG

1 egg, beaten	1/3 C milk
1/2 C vegetable oil	2 C flour
3 tsp baking powder	1½ C chopped figs
1/2 tsp salt	1/4 tsp cinnamon
1 C mashed banana	1/4 C brown sugar

Beat together egg, milk, oil. Stir in other ingredients until mixture is moist and lumpy. Fill 12 muffin cups 3/4 full; bake at 400o for 20-25 minutes.

BANANAS FOSTER

2½ C flour	3/4 C brown sugar
1¼ tsp baking soda	1 tsp baking powder
1½ C bananas, mashed	3/4 C milk
1/2 C sour cream	1 egg, beaten
1 tsp vanilla extract	2 tbs rum extract (or rum)

* * *

Optional Topping: 1/4 C margarine melted, 1/4 C brown sugar, 1/4 C rum. In saucepan, blend sugar with margarine. Remove from heat, stir in rum.

Combine dry ingredients. In another bowl, mix wet ingredients, blend into dry. Fill 12 greased muffin cups 3/4 full, bake 15-20 minutes at 375o. While muffins are hot in cups, puncture tops with fork, drizzle topping over tops.

BANANA OATMEAL

1 C rolled oats	1 C milk
2 C flour	1 tsp baking soda
1¼ C sugar	5 tsp baking powder
1/2 tsp salt	1/2 tsp cinnamon
1/4 tsp nutmeg	1/2 C margarine (melted)
2 eggs	2 tsp vanilla extract
2 C mashed bananas (mash with fork; 4-5 bananas)	

Combine oats and milk; set aside. In bowl, mix dry ingredients. To oats, add eggs, margarine, vanilla, bananas; combine mixtures, moisten. Fill 12 greased cups 2/3; 375o for 20 minutes (until golden brown).

BANANA ORANGE

1 egg, beaten	1/3 C milk
1/4 C vegetable oil	2 C flour
1/2 C sugar	3 tsp baking powder
1/2 tsp salt	1/2 C orange juice
3/4 C wheat germ	1 C mashed bananas

Combine egg, milk, oil. Stir in other ingredients until mixture is moist and lumpy. Fill 12 greased cups 3/4 full, bake at 400o 20-25 minutes.

BASIC

These muffins are quick, easy, and can be whipped up for unexpected breakfast or dinner guests.

1 egg, beaten	3/4 C milk
1/2 C vegetable oil	1/4 C sugar
3 tsp baking powder	1/2 tsp salt
2 C flour	

Combine egg, milk, oil; stir in other ingredients, mix into a lumpy batter. Fill 12 greased tins 3/4 full, bake at 400o for 20-25 minutes.

BEER

Serve these with crabs or at
an Oktoberfest meal!

3 C flour	1/2 tsp salt
3 tbs sugar	1 bottle beer
5 tsp baking powder	

Put dry ingredients in large bowl,
pour beer over, blend. Fill 12
greased tins 2/3 full, brush with
margarine. 350o 15-20 minutes.

BLACKBERRY MEADOW

My father made the best blackberry cobbler this side
of creation. These muffins come a close second to
Daddy's cobbler.

1 1/3 C flour	1/3 C sugar
1/2 tsp salt	2 tsp baking powder
1/4 C vegetable oil	3/4 C rolled oats
1 egg, beaten	3/4 C milk
1½ C blackberries, fresh or frozen (thaw, pat dry)	

Combine dry ingredients; in another bowl, mix milk,
egg, margarine, berries; combine mixtures well.
Fill 12 greased tins 3/4 full, 400o 20-25 minutes.

BLACK FOREST

Visions of Bavaria, castles, forests (and gnomes)
will dance in your head as you savor these sweeties.

1/4 C margarine
3 squares (1 oz each) unsweetened chocolate
2 eggs, separated   1½ C sugar
2¼ C sifted cake flour   2 tsp baking powder
1/2 tsp salt   1 1/3 C milk
8 oz package cream cheese, very soft
1 large jar cherry preserves

Melt margarine and chocolate (don't boil); pour in
large bowl, add eggs and sugar, stir well. Add
flour, baking powder, salt, cheese; slowly add milk,

stir. Fill 18 greased cups 1/3 full, spoon 1/2 tbs of preserves completely over batter; fill cups to 2/3 and bake at 375o for 25 minutes.

BLACK WALNUT

<u>Only</u> black walnuts will do in this muffin.

1 egg, beaten	3/4 C milk
1/2 C vegetable oil	1/4 C sugar
3 tsp baking powder	1/2 tsp salt
2 C flour	1 C chopped black walnuts

Combine egg, milk, oil; stir in other ingredients, mix into a lumpy batter. Fill 12 greased tins 3/4 full; bake at 400o for 20-25 minutes.

BLUEBERRY

1 C fresh or frozen (patted dry) blueberries
2 C flour   1/4 C sugar
1 tbs plus 1 tsp baking powder
1 C milk   1 egg
2 tbs vegetable oil   1/4 tsp salt

Combine flour, sugar, baking powder. In another
bowl, beat milk, egg, oil; add to dry items, stir
until just moistened; fold in blueberries. Fill
12 greased tins 3/4 full; bake at 400o 25 minutes.
Variations of the Blueberry recipe:
BLUEBERRY COCONUT - Add 3/4 C coconut
BLUEBERRY CRANBERRY - Replace the 1 C blueberries
with 1/2 C blueberries and 1/2 C cranberries.

<u>BLUEBERRY PINEAPPLE</u> – Replace the 1 C blueberries with 1/2 C blueberries and 4 oz crushed pineapple (drained).

BLUEBERRY STREUSEL

1/4 C sugar   1/4 C margarine, melted
1 egg, beaten   2 1/3 C flour
1 tbs plus 1 tsp baking powder
1/4 tsp salt   1 C milk
1 tsp vanilla extract
1 C blueberries fresh or frozen (thaw, pat dry)
         *   *   *
Streusel topping: 1/2 C sugar, 1/2 tsp cinnamon,
1/4 C nuts, 1/4 C margarine, melted

Fluff sugar and margarine, add egg. In another
bowl, mix flour, baking powder, salt; add to wet
mixture alternately with milk, stir well. Stir in
vanilla, fold in berries. Fill 15 greased tins 2/3

full. Combine topping items, cut in butter until crumbly; sprinkle on batter. Bake at 375o for 20 minutes.

BOYSENBERRY

2 C flour   1/4 C sugar
1 tbs+1 tsp baking powder
1 C milk   1 egg, beaten
2 tbs vegetable oil
1 C boysenberries

Combine dry items. In
another bowl, mix wet
ingredients, blend with
dry, fold in berries,
fill tins 2/3 full;
400o for 25 minutes.

BRAN

2¾ C bran	2¾ tsp baking soda
1/2 tsp salt	1 1/3 C whole wheat flour
2 eggs (or 4 egg whites)	2/3 C buttermilk
1/3 C vegetable oil	1/3 C dark molasses
1/4 C honey	1/4 tsp cinnamon (opt)
1 C raisins (opt)	1/2 C chopped nuts (opt)

Blend bran, flour, baking soda, salt, spice; add eggs, buttermilk, oil, molasses, honey; mix well; stir in raisins and nuts. Fill 12 greased tins 2/3 full; bake at 375o for 12-15 minutes.

CARIBBEAN

Get ready to go on a trip to a tropical paradise!
The islands come alive with these lively muffins.

2½ C bran
2½ tsp baking soda
3/4 C raisins
1 C shredded coconut
1/2 C buttermilk
1¼ C mashed banana

1 1/3 C flour
1/2 tsp salt
1/2 C chopped walnuts
2 eggs, beaten
1/2 C vegetable oil
1/2 C honey

Combine dry ingredients; in another bowl, mix wet
ingredients; blend mixtures together. Fill 15
greased tins 3/4 full; 375o for 20-25 minutes.

CAROB BANANA

1 egg, beaten	1/3 C milk
1 C mashed banana	1/2 C vegetable oil
2 C unbleached flour	1/4 C brown sugar
3 tsp baking powder	1/2 tsp salt
1½ C carob chips	1/2 C chopped nuts (opt)

Beat together egg, milk and oil. Stir in other
items to a moist and lumpy batter. Fill 12 greased
tins 3/4 full; bake at 400o 20-25 minutes.

CAROB CHIP

1½ C carob chips
2 C unbleached flour
1/4 C sugar
1/4 tsp salt
1 tbs+1 tsp baking powder
1 C milk
1 egg (or 2 whites)
2 tbs vegetable oil
1/2 C chopped nuts (opt)

Combine dry ingredients;
add wet items, moisten;
fold in chips; 12 greased
tins 3/4 full; 400o for
20-25 minutes.

CARROT

1 C whole wheat (or unbleached white) flour	
3/4 C oat bran	2 tsp baking powder
1/2 tsp cinnamon	1/4 tsp allspice
1/8 tsp nutmeg	1/4 tsp salt
2/3 C unsweetened orange juice	
1/4 C molasses	
4 egg whites (or 2 eggs)	
1/2 C finely grated carrot	
1/3 C raisins	1/3 C chopped nuts (opt)

Combine dry ingredients. In another bowl, whisk juice, molasses, oil, egg together; add dry mixture, then carrots, raisins, nuts. Fill 12 greased tins 3/4 full; bake at 375o for 20 minutes (until brown).

CARROTCAKE

3/4 C raisins	1/2 C water
1 3/4 C flour	1 tsp baking soda
1/8 tsp salt	3/4 tsp cinnamon
1/2 tsp allspice	1 egg
1/2 C sugar	1/4 C vegetable oil
1/4 tsp vanilla extract	1/4 tsp lemon extract
1 C unsweetened applesauce	
1 C grated carrots	1/2 C chopped nuts (opt)

Combine raisins and warm water, let set; in another

bowl, combine dry ingredients. In another bowl,
fluff egg and sugar; add oil, extracts, applesauce;
blend into flour mixture, fold in carrots, raisins,
water. Fill 12 greased tins 3/4 full; 400o for
15-20 minutes until golden brown.

CARROT SPICE

2 C flour
1 tsp baking soda
1/2 tsp nutmeg
1/3 C milk
2 C grated carrot
1/3 C chopped nuts (opt)

2 tsp baking powder
3/4 tsp cinnamon
1/3 C honey
1 egg
1/3 C golden raisins

Combine flour, baking powder, baking soda, spices;
mix well; add honey, milk, egg, carrot, blend; fold
in raisins and nuts. Fill 12 greased tins 3/4 full;
bake at 350o for 15-18 minutes.

CHEESE

2 C flour
2½ tsp baking powder
1 C buttermilk
6 tbs butter, melted

1/4 C sugar
1/2 tsp salt
1 C cheddar cheese
1 egg, beaten

Combine dry ingredients; add wet ingredients, mix.
Fill 12 greased tins 3/4 full; bake at 400o for
20 minutes.

CHERRIES JUBILEE

1 egg, beaten
3/4 C milk
1/2 C vegetable oil
2 C flour
1/4 C sugar
3 tsp baking powder
1/2 tsp salt
8 oz pkg cream cheese, soft
1 C cherries fresh or frozen

Combine egg, milk, oil, cheese;
stir in other items to a lumpy
batter. Fill 12 greased tins
3/4 full; 400o 20-25 minutes.

CHERRY

1¼ C cherries fresh or frozen
1 3/4 C flour   3/4 C sugar
1 tbs plus 1 tsp baking powder
1/4 tsp salt   1/2 C oil
2 eggs, beaten   1/2 C chopped pecans (opt)

Combine dry ingredients; add oil and eggs, blend.
Add nuts and cherries; blend until moistened. Fill
12 greased tins 2/3 full; 400o for 20-25 minutes.
Variation:
CHERRY COCONUT - Add 1 C coconut

CHOCOLATE (BASIC)

1/4 C margarine
3 squares (1 oz each) unsweetened chocolate
2 eggs, separated   1½ C sugar
2¼ C sifted cake flour   2 tsp baking powder
1/4 tsp salt   1 1/3 C milk

Melt margarine and chocolate (don't boil), pour in
bowl, add eggs, then sugar, blend well. Add dry
ingredients, mix; slowly add milk, stir after each
addition. Fill 12 greased tins 3/4 full; bake at
375o for 20-25 minutes.

Variations of the Basic Chocolate recipe:

CHOCOLATE ALMOND BLISS – Add 1 C coconut, 2 tbs almond extract and 1/2 C chopped almonds to Chocolate recipe.

CHOCOLATE BUTTERSCOTCH – Add 6 oz butterscotch chips to Chocolate recipe.

CHOCOLATE CARAMEL – Add 1 14 oz pkg caramels (melt caramels in 1½ tbs milk – don't boil) to Chocolate recipe.

CHOCOLATE CHOCOLATE – Add 1 12 oz pkg chocolate chips to Chocolate recipe.

CHOCOLATE COCONUT – Add 1 C coconut and 2 tbs coconut extract to Chocolate recipe.

CHOCOLATE MACADAMIA – Add 1 C chopped macadamia nuts to Chocolate recipe.

CHOCOLATE MINT – Add 2½ tbs mint extract to Chocolate recipe.

CHOCOLATE PEANUT BUTTER - Add 1 10 oz pkg peanut butter chips to Chocolate recipe.
CHOCOLATE RASPBERRY - Add 1 C raspberries, fresh or frozen (thaw, pat dry) to Chocolate recipe.
CHOCOLATE ZUCCHINI - Add 1 C well-shredded zucchini to Chocolate recipe.

CHOCOLATE CHEESECAKE

3 oz cream cheese
2 tbs sugar   1 C flour
3 tbs unsweet cocoa powder
2 tbs baking powder
1/2 C sugar   1 egg
3/4 C milk   1/3 C oil

Fluff cheese, 2 tbs sugar;
add dry items. Combine
wet items, add to dry,
moisten. Spoon 2 tbs
batter in greased tins,
drop 1 tsp cheese on top,
then a dab more batter.
375o for 20 minutes.

CHOCOLATE CHIP

2 C flour   1/4 C sugar
1 tbs plus 1 tsp baking powder
1/4 tsp salt   1 C milk
1 egg   2 tbs vegetable oil
pinch of cinnamon
12 oz pkg chocolate chips   1/2 chopped nuts (opt)

Combine flour, sugar, baking powder, salt, cinnamon.
Add milk, egg, oil; stir until moistened; fold in
chips. Fill 12 greased tins 3/4 full. Bake at
400o 20-25 minutes.

CHOCOLATE CREAM

1 egg, beaten	1/2 C milk
1/2 C vegetable oil	2 C flour
1/4 C sugar	3 tsp baking powder
1/4 tsp salt	8 oz sour cream
1/2 C unsweetened cocoa powder	
pinch of cinnamon	1/2 tsp baking soda

Combine egg, milk and oil; stir in remaining ingredients, mix into a lumpy batter. Fill 12 greased tins 3/4 full; 400o for 20-25 minutes.

CHOCOLATE DOUBLE TROUBLE

1 egg, beaten
1/2 C vegetable oil
1/2 C brown sugar
1/2 tsp salt
6 oz white chocolate chips

3/4 C milk
2 C flour
3 tsp baking powder
6 oz chocolate chips
3/4 C walnuts

Combine egg, milk and oil. Add everything else, and mix into a lumpy batter. Fill 12 greased tins 3/4 full; bake at 400o for 20-25 minutes.

CHOCOLATE FRANCAIS

1/4 C margarine
3 squares (1 oz each) white chocolate
2 eggs, separated   1½ C sugar
2½ C sifted cake flour   2 tsp baking powder
1/4 tsp salt   1 1/3 C milk
1 C raspberries fresh or frozen (thaw, pat dry)

Melt margarine and chocolate (don't boil); put in large bowl. Add eggs, blend; add sugar, stir. Add other ingredients, moisten well. Fill 12 greased tins 3/4 full; bake at 375o for 20-25 minutes.

CHOCOLATE PISTACHIO

1½ C flour
1 4 1/2 serving package of pistachio pudding
1/4 C unsweetened cocoa powder
2/3 C light brown sugar   1 tbs baking powder
1 3/4-2 C buttermilk   1 egg
1½ tsp vanilla extract   1/8 tsp salt
1/2 C chopped pistachios

Combine flour, pudding, baking powder, sugar. Add
other ingredients, stir until moist. Fill 12
greased tins 3/4 full; 375o for 20-25 minutes.

CHOCOLATE SUGAR-FREE

1 egg, beaten   3/4-1 C milk
1/2 C vegetable oil   2 C flour
3 tsp baking powder   1/2 tsp salt
1 4½ servings package sugar-free chocolate pudding

Combine egg, milk and oil, and pudding. Stir in
remaining ingredients; mix well. Fill 12 greased
tins 3/4 full, bake at 400o 20-25 minutes.

CHOCOLATE SWISS ALPINE

These Swiss muffins will make you want to yodel!

1/4 C margarine
3 squares (1 oz each) unsweetened <u>white</u> chocolate
2 eggs, separated   1½ C sugar
2¼ C sifted cake flour   2 tsp baking powder
1/4 tsp salt   1 1/3 C milk
3/4 to 1 C chopped hazelnuts

Melt margarine and chocolate (don't boil), pour in
large bowl, add eggs, stir; add sugar, mix well.
Add remaining ingredients, blend well. Fill 12
greased tins 3/4 full; bake at 375o 20-25 minutes.

CINNAMON RAISIN

1 egg, beaten	3/4 C milk
1/2 C vegetable oil	2 C flour
1/4 C sugar	3 tsp baking powder
1/2 tsp salt	1 tsp cinnamon
3/4 C dark raisins	

Combine egg, milk, oil; add other items, mix to a moist, lumpy batter. Fill 12 greased tins 3/4 full; bake at 400o 20-25 minutes (until golden). Sprinkle tops with sugar immediately.

COFFEE

1½ C flour
2¼ tsp baking powder
1 C chopped nuts
1/2 tsp cinnamon
3 tbs margarine
2/3 C strong coffee
1/4 C brown sugar
1 egg

Combine dry items; melt margarine with coffee and sugar; let cool a mite, add to dry mix, stir, add egg. Fill 12 greased tins 1/2; 375o 20-25 minutes.

75

COCONUT

These are wonderful party or brunch muffins --
perfect candidates for delicate miniatures!

2 C flour	1/4 tsp salt
4 tsp baking powder	1/4 C sugar
3 tsp margarine, melted	1 egg, beaten
1 C milk	1 C coconut
1/2 C finely chopped pecans	
shredded coconut (to garnish tops)	

Combine dry ingredients; mix wet items in another
bowl, add to dry mixture; add coconut, mix. Fill
10 greased standard tins 2/3 full; 4500 for 15
minutes (less for miniatures).

CORN
(Can be sugar-free)

1½ C yellow cornmeal   1/2 C flour
4 tsp baking powder   1/2 tsp salt
1 C milk   1 egg, beaten
1/4 C vegetable oil   2 tbs sugar (opt)
1/2 tsp cayenne pepper (opt)

Combine dry ingredients. In another bowl, mix wet
ingredients, add to dry mixture. Stir _only_ enough
to mix. Fill 12 greased tins 1/2 full; bake at
425o for 15-20 minutes.

CORN, TEXAS-STYLE

3 C flour
3 eggs, beaten
1 2/3 C buttermilk
1/2 C oil
1 can cream-style corn
1 tsp chili powder
2 onions, chopped
1½ C Longhorn cheese
2 tbs sugar

Mix in order given; 400o
20-25 minutes in greased
tins (until light brown).

CRAB

1 egg, beaten	1/2 C milk
1/2 C vegetable oil	2 C flour
3 tsp baking powder	dash of salt
8 oz sour cream	6 oz crabmeat
1-1½ tbs Old Bay (to taste)	

Combine egg, milk, oil, sour cream, salt, crab, Old Bay; add other ingredients, blend well. Fill 12 greased tins 3/4 full; 400o for 20-25 minutes.

CRANBERRY

Nice for Thanksgiving and Christmas!

1/4 C sugar	1/2 tsp salt

1 tbs plus 1 tsp baking powder

1 egg, beaten	3/4 C milk
1/4 C margarine, melted	2 C flour

1 C cranberries fresh or frozen (thaw, pat dry)

Combine dry ingredients, make a well in center. In

80

another bowl, combine wet items and berries, pour
in well, stir to moisten. Fill 12 greased tins 2/3
full and bake at 400o for 25-30 minutes.
Variations of the Cranberry recipe:
CRANBERRY APPLE - Substitute 1/2 C cranberries and
1/2 C chopped apples for the 1 C cranberries in the
Cranberry recipe.

CRANBERRY CHEDDAR - Add 1/2 C shredded cheddar cheese to the Cranberry recipe.

CRANBERRY ORANGE - Add 1/4 C unsweetened orange juice to the Cranberry recipe, and less milk to 1/2 C.

CRANBERRY PEAR - Substitute 1/2 C cranberries and 1/2 C chopped pear for the 1 C cranberries in the Cranberry recipe; add 1 tbs lemon juice.

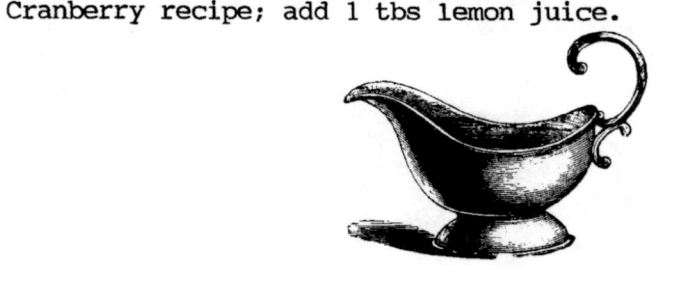

DATE

1¼ C buckwheat flour
1/2 C flour
1/2 C sugar
1 tsp baking powder
1/2 tsp baking soda
pinch of salt
1 C chopped dates
1 C buttermilk
3 tbs vegetable oil
1 egg, beaten

Combine first six items;
add dates, toss to coat;
add wet ingredients until
moist. Fill 12 greased
tins 3/4 full; 400o for
15 minutes.

DATE ORANGE

1¼ C whole wheat flour
1/2 C sugar
1/2 tsp baking soda
1 C chopped dates
1/2 C orange juice
1 egg, beaten

1/2 C flour
1 tsp baking powder
1/4 tsp salt
1/2 C buttermilk
3 tbs vegetable oil
1/2 C chopped nuts (opt)

Combine first six ingredients. Add dates, toss to coat; stir in wet ingredients until moist. Fill 12 greased tins 3/4 full, bake at 400o for 15 minutes.

EGGNOG

Happy holidays!

1 egg, beaten
1/2 C vegetable oil
1/2 C brown sugar
1/2 tsp salt
1 tsp vanilla extract
3 tbs rum extract (or rum)

1/2 C milk
2 C flour
3 tsp baking powder
$1\frac{1}{4}$ tsp nutmeg
1/2 C plain yogurt

Combine egg, milk and oil; stir in remaining
ingredients, mix into a lumpy batter. Fill 12
greased tins 3/4; bake at 400o 20-25 minutes.

ELDERBERRY

1 3/4 C flour
3/4 C sugar
1 tbs plus 1 tsp baking powder
1/2 tsp salt
1/2 C vegetable oil
2 eggs, beaten
1 C elderberries

Combine dry items; add oil, eggs; mix until moist;
fold in berries. Fill 12 greased tins 3/4 full; bake
at 375o for 20-25 minutes.

FIESTA

These playful muffins add zest to Mexican meals!

1¾ C yellow cornmeal	1/2 C flour
4 tsp baking powder	1/2 tsp salt
1 C milk	1 egg, beaten
1/4 C vegetable oil	1/4 tsp cayenne pepper
2 tbs sugar (opt)	1/2 C salsa

Mix cornmeal, flour, baking powder, salt. In another bowl, mix together milk, egg, oil, pepper, sugar and salsa. Combine with dry mixture; fill 12 greased tins 2/3 full and bake at 425º 15-20 minutes.

FIG

1 3/4 C chopped figs
1 egg, beaten
3/4 C milk
1/2 C vegetable oil
2 C flour
1/4 C sugar
3 tsp baking powder
1/2 tsp salt

Combine egg, milk, oil;
add other items, mix into
a lumpy batter. Fill 12
greased tins 3/4 full;
400o for 20-25 minutes.

FRENCH TOAST

1 egg, beaten	3/4 C milk
1/2 C vegetable oil	2 C flour
1/4 C sugar	3 tsp baking powder
1/4 tsp salt	

* * *

Topping: 1/4 C sugar, 3/4 tsp cinnamon, 1/4 C melted margarine (do not combine with sugar and spice)

Combine egg, milk, oil; add other ingredients, mix into a lumpy batter. Fill 12 greased tins 3/4 full; bake at 400º 20-25 minutes. While muffins are hot, brush tops with margarine, sprinkle with topping.

FRUIT BRAN

1½ C <u>whole</u> bran cereal (not flakes)
1/2 C boiling water   1 egg, beaten
1 C buttermilk   1/2 C honey
1/4 C melted margarine (or vegetable oil)
1½ C mixed dry fruit   1/2 C chopped nuts
1/2 C whole wheat flour   3/4 C white flour
1/4 tsp salt   1¼ tsp baking soda

Moisten cereal and water in large bowl, cool to
lukewarm; add wet ingredients and nuts; blend.
In another bowl, mix dry ingredients; combine
mixtures, stir to moisten. Fill 12 greased tins
3/4 full; bake at 425o for 20-25 minutes.

FRUITCAKE

Served with eggnog, this is a tasty holiday treat.

1 egg, beaten	3/4 C milk
1/2 C vegetable oil	2 C flour
1/4 C light brown sugar	3 tsp baking powder
1/4 tsp salt	3/4 C candied fruit

Combine egg, milk, oil; add other ingredients and stir into a lumpy batter. Fill 12 greased tins 3/4 full and bake at 400o for 20-25 minutes.

GINGER

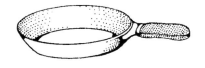

1 C shortening
3/4 C sugar
1 C waffle syrup
3 eggs
1 C buttermilk
1 3/4 tsp baking soda
2½ tsp ginger
1/4 tsp salt
3 C flour

Cream shortening and sugar; add eggs, syrup, then milk with baking soda dissolved in it. Add flour, spices, mix well. Fill 12 greased tins 3/4; 375o 10-12 minutes.

GINGER PEAR

1 egg, beaten
1/2 vegetable oil
1/4 C sugar
1/2 tsp salt
1/2 C chopped pear

3/4 C milk
2 C flour
3 tsp baking powder
2½ tsp ginger

Combine wet ingredients; add remaining ingredients, stir to a lumpy batter.   Fill 12 greased tins 3/4 full; bake at 400o for 20 minutes.
Variation: **GINGER PECAN** - Substitute 3/4 C chopped pecans for the pears.

GINGERBREAD

2½ C flour
1 C molasses
1/2 C margarine, melted
1½ tsp baking soda
1 tsp cinnamon

1/3 C sugar
3/4 C hot water
1 egg, beaten
2 tsp ground ginger
1/4 tsp salt

Combine flour, sugar, baking soda, salt and spices.
Add remaining ingredients, mix well. Fill 12 greased
tins 3/4 full; bake at 400o for 20-25 minutes.

GINGERBREAD CHOCOLATE

2 C flour	1/3 C sugar
1 C molasses	3/4 C hot water
1/2 C magarine, melted	1 egg, beaten
1½ tsp baking soda	2 tsp ground ginger
1 tsp cinnamon	1/4 tsp salt
1/3 C unsweetened cocoa powder	

Combine dry ingredients; add remaining items, mix well. Fill 12 greased tins 3/4 full; bake at 4000 for 20-25 minutes.

GOOSEBERRY

1 egg, beaten
1/2 C vegetable oil
3 tsp baking powder
2 C flour
1 C gooseberries

3/4 C milk
1/4 C sugar
1/2 tsp salt

Combine egg, milk, oil; add other ingredients, mix
into a lumpy batter. Fill 12 greased tins 3/4 full;
bake at 400o for 20-25 minutes.

GRANOLA

1 egg, beaten	1/2 C milk
1/2 C vegetable oil	1 C whole wheat flour
2 tbs sugar	2 C granola
dash of salt	1/4 tsp cinnamon

Mix egg, milk, oil; stir in remaining ingredients, just until moistened. Fill 12 greased tins 3/4 full; bake at 4000 for 20 minutes (until golden brown).

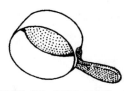

GRAPE NUT

During childhood summers spent on a Virginia farm, a big treat was eating homemade grape nut ice cream. These muffins bring back sweet Southern memories...

1¼ C flour
1/2 C sugar
1½ C Grape Nuts cereal
1 egg, beaten

3 tsp baking powder
1¼ C milk
¼ tsp nutmeg (opt)
1/3 C oil

Stir all ingredients together, fill greased tins 3/4 full. Bake at 400o for 25 minutes.

HAM

1 C yellow cornmeal	1 C flour
2 tbs sugar	2½ tsp baking powder
1 C buttermilk	6 tbs margarine, melted
1 egg, beaten	1/4 tsp salt
1 C cooked, cubed (½") ham	

Combine dry ingredients; add wet items, ham, mix well. Fill 12 greased tins 3/4 full; bake at 400o for 20-25 minutes (until lightly browned).

Variation: **HAM AND CHEESE** - Add 1 C shredded cheddar cheese.

HAWAIIAN

1 egg, beaten
1/2 C vegetable oil
1/4 C brown sugar
1 tsp vanilla extract
1/2 tsp salt
1/2 C coconut
6 oz white chocolate chips
1/2 C chopped macadamia nuts

3/4 C milk
2 C flour
3 tsp baking powder
1/2 tsp baking soda
6 oz chocolate chips

Combine egg, milk, oil; stir in other ingredients,
mix to a lumpy batter. Fill 12 greased tins 3/4 full;
bake at 400o for 20-25 minutes.

HAZELNUT

2 C flour	1/4 tsp salt
2 tsp baking powder	1/4 tsp allspice
3/4 tsp cinnamon	1/2 C dark brown sugar
1/4 C sugar	1/2 C margarine, melted
1 egg	1/2 tsp vanilla extract
1 C milk	1 C hazelnuts, ground

Mix flour, baking powder, salt, spices; make a well in center. In another bowl, fluff sugars and margarine; beat in egg, vanilla, milk; pour in well; blend; add nuts. Fill 12 greased tins 3/4 full; bake at 400o 15-20 minutes (until lightly browned).

HONEY

1 egg, beaten
3/4 C milk
1/2 C oil
2 C flour
1/3 C honey
3 tsp baking powder
1/2 tsp salt
3/4 C chopped nuts

Mix wet items, add
others, blend. Fill
12 greased tins 3/4,
400o 20-25 minutes.

HONEY APPLE

1 egg, beaten	3/4 C milk
1 medium apple, chopped	1/2 C vegetable oil
2 C flour	1/3 C honey
1/3 C light brown sugar	3 tsp baking powder
1/2 tsp salt	hint of allspice

Mix wet ingredients, add remaining items, blend well. Fill 12 greased tins 3/4 full; bake at 400o for 20-25 minutes (until golden brown).

IRISH

The batter will seem soupy, but don't worry --
these muffins are some of the best in this book.

2 C buttermilk	1 C rolled oats
2 eggs	1/3 C brown sugar
3/4 C whole wheat flour	1 tsp baking soda
1/4 tsp salt	2 tbs oil
1/4 tsp cinnamon (opt)	

Combine buttermilk and oatmeal six hours or
overnight (stir well, <u>cover</u>, refrigerate).   Beat
eggs in large bowl; add sugar, beat until smooth.
Add other ingredients; beat well.   Fill 6-9 greased
tins 3/4 full; bake at 400o for 15-20 minutes.

JAM SURPRISE

1 egg, beaten	3/4 C milk
1/2 C vegetable oil	2 C flour
1/4 C sugar	3 tsp baking powder
1/2 tsp salt	

strawberry, blueberry, or blackberry jam

Combine wet ingredients (except jam), add dry items;
mix to lumpy batter. Fill 12 greased tins 1/2 full,
spoon 1 tsp onto batter; top with batter to 3/4
full. Bake at 4000 for 20-25 minutes.

KAHLUA AND CREAM

1 egg, beaten	3/4 C milk
1/2 C vegetable oil	2 C flour
1/4 C sugar	3 tsp baking powder
1/2 tsp salt	3 tbs Kahlua
8 oz package of cream cheese, very soft	

Combine egg, milk, oil, kahlua, cream cheese. Stir in remaining items; mix to lumpy batter. Fill 12 greased tins 3/4 full; bake at 400o 20-25 minutes.

KEY LIME

1 egg, beaten
1/4 C milk
1/2 C vegetable oil
2 C flour
1/4 C sugar
3 tsp baking powder
1/2 tsp salt
1 pkg lime pudding
1/4 C lime juice

Combine wet ingredients;
add rest; stir to lumpy;
fill 12 greased tins 3/4;
400o 20-25 minutes.

LADY BALTIMORE

1 egg, beaten
1/2 C vegetable oil
1/4 C sugar
1/2 tsp salt
1/2 tsp almond extract
1/2 tsp vanilla extract
1 8 oz package dried figs, chopped

1 C milk
2 C flour
3 tsp baking powder
1/2 C chopped nuts
1/2 C raisins

Combine egg, milk, oil, extracts. Add remaining
items, stir to a lumpy batter. Fill 12 greased tins
3/4 full and bake at 400o for 20-25 minutes.

LANE

These delicate muffins are adapted from the famous
Southern Lane Cake.   They are perfect for miniatures.

1 egg, beaten	3/4 C milk
1/2 C vegetable oil	1/4 C sugar
3 tsp baking powder	1/2 tsp salt
2 C flour	1/2 C raisins
1/2 C chopped pecans (only pecans!!)	
3/4 C coconut	1 tsp vanilla extract
3/4 C chopped maraschino (or candied) cherries	

Combine egg, milk, oil; stir in other ingredients, mix
into a lumpy batter.   Fill 12 greased tins 3/4 full;
bake at 400o for 20 minutes.

LEMON

1 C flour	1 C rolled oats
1/2 C sugar	2 tsp baking powder
1 egg, beaten	2/3 C milk
2 tbs lemon juice	1/3 C oil

Combine dry ingredients, add wet items; blend. Fill
12 greased tins 2/3 full; bake at 400o 10-15 minutes.
Variation: **LEMON BLUEBERRY** - Add 3/4 C blueberries
(if frozen, thaw and pat dry) to Lemon recipe.

LEMON POPPYSEED

1 egg, beaten	1/2 C milk
1/2 C vegetable oil	2 C flour
1/4 C sugar	3 tsp baking powder
1/2 tsp salt	1 tbs poppy seeds
3/4 C sour cream	1/4 C lemon juice
1 tsp vanilla extract	

Combine dry ingredients, make a well in center; pour remaining items into bowl, moisten well. Fill 12 greased tins 1/2 full; bake at 400o 20-25 minutes.

LEMON RASPBERRY

1 egg, beaten   3/4 C milk
1/2 C vegetable oil   2 C flour
1/4 C sugar   3 tsp baking powder
1/2 tsp salt   2 tbs lemon extract
3/4 C raspberries fresh or frozen (thaw, pat dry)

Combine egg, milk and oil; stir in remaining items,
mix to a lumpy batter. Fill 12 greased tins 3/4
full; bake at 400o for 20-25 minutes.

LOVERS' SECRET

Very sinful and decadent!

1/4 C margarine

3 squares (1 oz each) unsweetened chocolate

2 eggs, separated   1½ C sugar

2¾ C sifted cake flour   2 tsp baking powder

1/4 tsp salt   1 1/3 C milk

6 oz white chocolate chips

1/2 C macadamia nuts, chopped

Melt margarine and chocolate (don't boil); pour in large bowl; add eggs, sugar; mix well; add other ingredients slowly, mix well. Fill 12 greased tins 3/4 full; bake at 375o for 20-25 minutes.

MACADAMIA

1½ C flour
1/2 C sugar
1 C chopped macadamias
2 tsp baking powder
1/4 tsp salt
1/4 tsp nutmeg
1 egg, beaten
1/2 C milk
1/4 C vegetable oil

Combine first six items, make well in center; in another bowl mix wet items, pour in well, moisten. Fill 12 greased tins 3/4 full; 400o for 20-25 minutes.

MARMALADE

This is the perfect breakfast muffin with a cup
of tea.

1¼ C unbleached flour   1 C wheat bran
1 tbs baking powder   pinch of salt
3/4 C plain yogurt   1/8 tsp ginger
1 egg   1 tsp vanilla
1½ C + 1 tbs orange marmalade

Combine dry ingredients; stir well. Add other
items; stir to moisten. Fill 12 greased tins
3/4 full; bake at 350o for 15-18 minutes.

MEXICAN

1¼ C flour
1 tbs sugar
1/4 tsp salt
1/4 tsp ground red pepper
2 tbs margarine, melted
1/2 C diced red bell pepper
1/2 C sliced green onion
3/4 tsp seeded minced jalapeno pepper

3/4 C yellow cornmeal
2 tsp baking powder

1 C buttermilk
1 egg, beaten lightly

Combine first six ingredients in large bowl, make a
well in center. In another bowl, combine buttermilk,
margarine, egg and pour in well, stir to moisten;
fold in bell pepper, onions and jalapeno. Fill 12
greased tins 3/4 full; 400o for 20-25 minutes.

MINCEMEAT

2 C flour	1/3 C sugar
3/4 C chopped pecans or walnuts	
2 tsp baking powder	1/4 tsp salt
1/4 tsp nutmeg	1/2 tsp cinnamon
1/3 C milk	2 eggs
1½ C prepared mincemeat	

Mix flour, nuts, sugar, baking powder, salt, spices. In another bowl, beat milk and eggs; add to dry mixture along with mincemeat; blend well. Fill 12 greased tins 3/4 full; bake at 400O for 15-20 minutes.

MIXED BERRY

1/3 C blueberries fresh or frozen (thaw, pat dry)
1/3 C blackberries fresh or frozen (thaw, pat dry)
1/3 C raspberries fresh or frozen (thaw, pat dry)

1/4 C sugar   1/4 tsp salt
1 tbs + 1 tsp baking powder   2 C flour
1 egg, beaten   3/4 C milk
1/4 C margarine, melted

Combine flour, sugar, baking powder, salt; make
a well in center. In another bowl, combine egg,
milk, butter; pour into well; fold in berries, stir
to moisten. Fill 12 greased tins 2/3 full; bake at
400o for 25-30 minutes.

MULTI-GRAIN

1/2 C cornmeal
1/4 C regular oats, uncooked
2 tbs sugar
1¼ tsp baking powder
1/4 C vegetable oil

1/4 C unbleached flour
1½ tsp wheat germ
1/4 tsp salt
1/2 C buttermilk
1 egg, beaten

Combine cornmeal, oats, flour, wheat germ; stir in sugar, baking powder and salt. Add buttermilk, oil and egg, stir to a lumpy batter. Fill 10 greased tins 2/3 full; bake at 375o for 20-25 minutes.

NUTMEG WALNUT

1 egg, beaten
3/4 C milk
1/2 C vegetable oil
2 C flour
1/4 C sugar
3 tsp baking powder
1/2 tsp salt
1 tbs nutmeg
3/4 C chopped walnuts

Combine wet items; add
other ingredients; mix
to lumpy batter. Fill
12 greased tins 3/4;
400o 20-25 minutes.

OATMEAL

1½ C whole wheat flour	2 tsp baking powder
1/2 tsp salt	3/4 C rolled oats
1 C milk	1 egg
3 tbs margarine, melted	2 tbs molasses
1/2 C currants (or raisins)	1/2 tsp cinnamon

Sift together flour, baking powder, salt; add oats.
In another bowl, beat milk, eggs, margarine,
molasses; add currants. Combine mixtures, stir well.
Fill 12 greased tins 3/4 full; bake at 400o for
20-25 minutes.

Variation: OATMEAL COCONUT - Add 3/4 C shredded coconut
and 1/2 C chopped nuts to Oatmeal recipe; omit raisins.

ONION

1 C chopped onions	1 C flour
1 C rye flour	1 egg, beaten
3/4 C milk	1/2 C vegetable oil
1/4 C sugar	3 tsp baking powder
1/2 tsp salt	2 tbs margarine

Cook onions in margarine until soft; in a large bowl, combine egg, milk, oil. Add remaining ingredients, mix into a lumpy batter. Fill 12 greased tins 3/4 full and bake at 400o for 20-25 minutes.

ORANGE

1 C flour	2 tsp baking powder
1/4 tsp nutmeg	1 egg, beaten
1½ tsp margarine, melted	1/2 C milk
1/3 C packed brown sugar	1/4 tsp salt

grated rind and juice of 1 orange

Combine flour, baking powder, salt, nutmeg. Add margarine, egg, milk and sugar, stir to moisten; blend in juice and rind. Fill 12 greased tins 2/3 full; bake at 400o for 20-22 minutes.

PAIN KILLER

These muffins are adapted from a Caribbean drink.

1 egg, beaten	1/4 C milk
1/2 C vegetable oil	2 C flour
1/4 C brown sugar	3 tsp baking powder
1/4 tsp salt	4 oz orange juice
1 8 oz can crushed pineapple (partially drained)	
1 C shredded coconut	3 tbs rum extract

Combine dry ingredients; add remaining ingredients, stir to a lumpy batter. Fill 12 greased tins 3/4 full and bake at 400o for 20-25 minutes.

PARMESAN CORN

3 3/4 C milk	1½ C yellow cornmeal
3 eggs, beaten	1/4 tsp cayenne pepper
1/4 tsp salt	4 tbs margarine
1 C grated Parmesan cheese	2 tbs sugar (opt)

Heat milk to just below boiling; reduce heat to
medium, stir in cornmeal, stir constantly for five
minutes until thick. Remove from heat; beat in eggs;
add other items (sprinkle some cheese on muffins).
Fill 12 greased tins 3/4 full; 425o for 20-25 minutes.

PARMESAN HERB

These muffins are excellent with Italian food.

1 egg, beaten   3/4 C buttermilk
1/2 C vegetable oil   2 C flour
1/4 C sugar   3 tsp baking powder
1/2 tsp salt   1/4 C chopped parsley
1/4 tsp sage   1/8 tsp basil
3/4 C grated Parmesan cheese

Combine milk, egg, oil; stir in other ingredients,
mix to a lumpy batter. Fill 12 greased tins 3/4
full; bake at 400o for 20-25 minutes.

PEACH

1¼ C peaches
3/4 C sugar
1/4 tsp salt
1 tbs+1 tsp baking powder

1 3/4 C flour
1/4 tbs nutmeg
1/2 C vegetable oil
2 eggs, beaten

Combine dry ingredients; add oil and egg, blend to
moisten; fold in peaches. Fill 12 greased tins 2/3
full; bake at 375o for 20-25 minutes.

PEANUT BUTTER AND CHOCOLATE CHIP

2 C flour
1/3 C chunky peanut butter
1 tsp salt
2 eggs, beaten
12 oz package of chocolate chips

1/4 C sugar
1 tbs baking powder
1 C milk
2 tbs vegetable oil

Combine flour and sugar in large bowl; cut in peanut
butter until mixture looks like coarse meal.   In
another bowl, combine remaining ingredients, beat;
combine mixtures, moisten. Fill 12 greased tins
3/4 full; bake at 400o for 20-25 minutes.

PEANUT BUTTER AND JELLY

1 3/4 C flour
2½ tsp baking powder
1/2 C creamy peanut butter
3/4 C milk
1/2 C grape or strawberry jelly

1/4 C sugar
1/2 tsp salt
1 egg, beaten
1/3 C margarine, melted

Combine dry ingredients. In another bowl, mix
peanut butter and egg, then milk, then butter; mix,
add to dry mixture, stir to stiff batter. Put
heaping tbs of batter in each greased tin, make
indentation with finger in center. Put tsp of jelly
in hole; cover with tbs of batter (tin should be
2/3 full); 375o for 20 minutes.

PEAR

1 C pears
1 3/4 C flour
1/2 C sugar
1/2 tsp cinnamon
1/2 tsp salt
1 tbs+1 tsp baking powder
1/2 C corn oil
2 eggs, beaten

Combine dry items; add
oil and egg, blend; add
pears; moisten mixture.
Fill 12 greased tins 2/3;
375o for 20-25 minutes.

PECAN

The thoroughly Southern pecan produces a delightful muffin.

1½ C flour	1/2 C sugar
1 C chopped pecans	2 tsp baking powder
1/2 tsp salt	1/4 tsp nutmeg
1 egg, beaten lightly	1/2 C milk
1/4 C vegetable oil	

Combine first six ingredients, make a well. In another bowl, combine wet ingredients; pour into well, stir to moisten. Fill 12 greased tins 2/3 full; bake for 20-25 minutes at 400o.

PINA COLADA

These lively muffins are every bit as good as their namesake tropical drink! They are wonderful for parties or dessert.

1 egg, beaten   1/2 C milk
1/2 C vegetable oil   2 C flour
1/4 C brown sugar   3 tsp baking powder
1/2 tsp salt   1 C shredded coconut
1 8 oz can crushed pineapple (partially drained)
3 tbs rum extract

Combine egg, milk, oil; add dry ingredients; fold in pineapple, coconut, rum extract; stir to moisten. Fill 12 greased tins 3/4; bake at 400o 20-25 minutes.

PINEAPPLE

2 C flour	2 tsp baking powder
1/2 tsp salt	1/2 C brown sugar
1/2 tsp baking soda	1 egg, beaten

1 8 oz can crushed pineapple (undrained)
1 8 oz carton sour cream
1/3 C margarine, melted
1/2 C chopped pecans or walnuts (opt)

Combine first five ingredients, make a well. Add other ingredients to well, moisten. Fill 12 greased tins 3/4 full; bake at 400o for 20-25 minutes.

PINEAPPLE CARROT

1 egg, beaten	1/2 C milk
1/2 C vegetable oil	2 C flour
1/4 C sugar	3 tsp baking powder
1/2 tsp salt	1/2 C shredded carrot
4 oz crushed pineapple (partially drained)	

Combine egg, milk, oil; stir in remaining items,
mix to a lumpy batter. Fill 12 greased tins 3/4
full; bake at 400o for 20-25 minutes.

PINEAPPLE PEAR

1 egg, beaten	3/4 C milk
1/2 C vegetable oil	2 C flour
1/4 C sugar	3 tsp baking powder
1/2 tsp salt	1/2 C pears
4 oz crushed pineapple (partially drained)	

Combine egg, milk, oil; stir in other ingredients, mix to a lumpy batter. Fill 12 greased tins 3/4 full; bake at 400o for 20-25 minutes.

PISTACHIO

1 egg, beaten	1½ C milk
1/2 C vegetable oil	2 C flour
1/4 C sugar	3 tsp baking powder
1/4 tsp salt	1 box pistachio pudding
1 C chopped pistachios (opt)	

Combine egg, milk and oil; add other items, mix
to a lumpy batter. Fill 12 greased tins 3/4 full;
bake at 400o for 20-25 minutes.

PLUM

1 C whole wheat flour
1/4 C unprocessed wheat bran
3/4 tsp baking soda
1 egg, beaten
1/8 C vegetable oil
1/2 tsp cinnamon
1½ C finely chopped plums

1/2 C rolled oats
1/4 C brown sugar
pinch of salt
3/4 C buttermilk
1½ tsp orange juice
1/8 tsp nutmeg

Combine and blend all ingredients. Fill 12 greased
tins 3/4 full; bake at 400o for 20-25 minutes.

PUMPKIN

3/4 C brown sugar	1/4 C molasses
1/2 C margarine, softened	1 egg, beaten
1 C canned pumpkin	1 3/4 C flour
1 tsp baking soda	1/8 tsp salt

Combine sugar, butter, molasses, beat well; add egg,
pumpkin, beat until smooth. In another bowl, mix other
ingredients; add to pumpkin, stir to moist, lumpy batter.
Fill 15 greased tins 1/2 full; 350o for 20-25 minutes.
Variations of Pumpkin recipe:
PUMPKIN APPLE - Add 1/2 C chopped apple to recipe.
PUMPKIN PECAN - Add 3/4 C chopped pecans to recipe.

PUMPKIN CHOCOLATE

2¼ C flour   2/3 C brown sugar
1/4 C unsweetened cocoa powder
pinch of salt   1 tbs baking powder
1½ C buttermilk   1 egg, beaten
1½ tsp vanilla extract   1 C canned pumpkin

Combine flour, cocoa, sugar, baking powder, mix; add
remaining ingredients, stir to moisten. Fill 12
greased tins 3/4; bake at 350o for 15-18 minutes.

PUMPKIN MAPLE

3/4 C brown sugar	1/4 C maple syrup
1/2 C margarine, softened	1 egg, beaten
1 C canned pumpkin	1 3/4 C flour
1 tsp baking soda	dash of salt
1/2 C chopped pecans or walnuts (opt)	

Combine sugar, butter, syrup, beat well. Add egg and
pumpkin, beat until smooth. Stir together remaining
ingredients, add to pumpkin mixture, stir to a moist
and lumpy batter. Fill 12 greased tins 1/2 full;
bake at 350o for 15-18 minutes.

PRUNE

1 egg, beaten
3/4 C milk
1/4 C oil
1 C flour
3/4 C wheat germ
1/4 C sugar
2 tsp baking powder
1/2 tsp salt
1 C chopped prunes

Blend egg, milk, oil.
Combine dry items,
add to wet mixture,
moisten. Fill 10
greased tins 2/3;
400o 20 minutes.

PRUNE BRAN

2¼ C bran	2½ tsp baking soda
1 1/3 C whole wheat (or unbleached white) flour	
1/4 tsp salt	2 eggs
2/3 C buttermilk	1/3 C vegetable oil
1/3 C dark molasses	1/4 C honey
1/8 tsp cinnamon	1 C chopped prunes

Blend bran, flour, baking soda, salt, cinnamon. Add remaining ingredients, blend well. Fill 12 greased tins 2/3 full; bake at 425o for 12-15 minutes.

QUICK-BE-GONES

1/2 C margarine, softened
1 egg
1 tsp vanilla extract
2 tsp unsweetened cocoa powder
1/2 tsp baking powder
1 C rolled oats, uncooked
6 oz chocolate chips

3/4 C brown sugar

1 C flour
pinch of salt
1/4 tsp baking soda
1/2 C raisins
3/4 C chopped nuts

Cream butter and sugar; add egg and vanilla, beat.
In another bowl, combine flour, cocoa, baking powder
and baking soda. Stir into sugar mixture with oats,
chips, raisins, nuts. Fill 12 greased tins 3/4 full
and bake at 400o 15-18 minutes.

RASPBERRY

1 C red raspberries fresh or frozen (thaw, pat dry)	
1/2 C milk	1/4 C oil
1 egg, beaten	1/2 C sugar
1½ C flour	2 tsp baking powder
1/2 tsp salt	

Combine milk, oil, egg; stir in flour, sugar, baking powder and salt to moisten; fold in berries. Fill 12 greased tins 2/3 full; bake at 4000 20-25 minutes.

RHUBARB

1 3/4 C diced rhubarb
1 egg, beaten
3/4 C buttermilk
1/2 C vegetable oil
2 C flour
1/4 C sugar
1 tsp baking soda
pinch of salt

Combine egg, milk, oil; stir in other ingredients to a
lumpy batter. Fill 12 greased tins 3/4 full; bake at
400o for 20-25 minutes.

Variation: **RHUBARB STRAWBERRY** - Substitute 3/4 C diced
rhubarb and 3/4 C strawberries for the 1 3/4 C rhubarb.

RUM

1 egg, beaten
3/4 C milk
1/2 C vegetable oil
2 C flour
1/4 C sugar
3 tsp baking powder
1/2 tsp salt
3 tbs rum extract (or rum)
1/2 C raisins

Combine egg, milk, oil;
stir in other ingredients
to a lumpy batter. Fill
12 greased tins 3/4 full;
400o 20-25 minutes.

RYE

These easy-to-make muffins go well with hearty, winter fare.

1 egg, beaten	3/4 C milk
1/2 C vegetable oil	2 C rye flour
1 tbs caraway seed	1/3 C sugar
3 tbs baking powder	1/2 tsp salt

Combine wet ingredients; add dry ingredients, mix to a moist, lumpy batter. Fill 12 greased tins 3/4 full; bake at 4000 for 20-25 minutes.

Variation: **RYE AND CHEESE:** Add 1 C shredded cheddar cheese.

RYE AND CORN

1 C whole wheat flour
1/4 C dark rye flour
3/4 tsp baking soda
1½ C buttermilk
1/4 C vegetable oil

3/4 C yellow cornmeal
1 tsp baking powder
1/4 tsp salt
1 egg
1/4 C honey

Sift together dry ingredients; beat wet ingredients
in a different bowl. Combine mixtures, stir well.
Fill 12 greased tins 2/3 full; 400o 20-25 minutes.

SAUSAGE

1½ C yellow cornmeal	1/2 C flour
4 tsp baking powder	1/2 tsp salt
1 C milk	1 egg, beaten
1/4 C vegetable oil	
1/4 lb cooked pork sausage	

Mix dry ingredients; combine wet ingredients and
sausage, add to dry mixture, stirring only to mix.
Fill 12 greased tins 1/2 full; bake at 425o for
15-20 minutes (until lightly browned).

Variation: **SAUSAGE AND CHEESE:** Add 1/2 C shredded
cheddar cheese.

SESAME
(SUGAR-FREE)

3 eggs
1/4 C margarine, softened
2/3 C apple juice (unsweetened)
2 C unbleached white flour   1 tsp baking powder
1/2 tsp baking soda   1/4 tsp salt
1/2 C sesame seeds

Beat together eggs, margarine, juice. Add flour,
baking powder; beat; add seeds. Fill 12 greased tins
3/4 full and sprinkle tops with seeds. Bake at 350o
for 10-12 minutes (until lightly browned).

SOUR CREAM

1 egg	3/4 C milk
1/2 C vegetable oil	2 C flour
1/4 C sugar	3 tsp baking powder
1/2 tsp salt	8 oz sour cream

Combine egg, milk, oil; add remaining ingredients, mix to a lumpy batter. Fill 12 greased tins 3/4 full; bake at 400o for 20-25 minutes.

Variation: **SOUR CREAM AND CHIVES:** Add 1/4 C chopped chives.

SPICED

2 eggs
3/4 C unsweetened orange juice
1 tsp vanilla extract
2 C 100% bran cereal
3/4 C whole wheat flour
2 tsp baking powder
1¼ tsp cinnamon
1/4 tsp ground cloves

1/4 C vegetable oil
1/3 C molasses
1/2 C raisins
1/2 C oat bran
1/4 C wheat germ
dash of salt
3/4 tsp nutmeg

Combine wet ingredients in large bowl; add cereal and raisins. Combine dry ingredients in another bowl; combine mixtures. Fill 12 greased tins 2/3 full; bake at 375o for 20-25 minutes.

SQUASH

Your favorite kind of squash can be used...

1 2/3 C flour	2 tsp baking powder
1½ tsp cinnamon	½ tsp allspice
1/2 tsp salt	2 eggs, beaten
1¼ C mashed cooked squash	3/4 C maple syrup
1/3 C vegetable oil	1 tsp vanilla
1/2 C chopped pecans	1/2 C raisins

Mix dry ingredients, make a well in center; in another bowl, combine wet ingredients; pour into well, stir to a moist, lumpy batter. Fold in nuts and raisins. Fill 15 greased tins 3/4 full; bake at 375o for 18-20 minutes.

STRAWBERRY

1¼ C fresh (cleaned, hulled) or frozen strawberries
1 3/4 C flour   3/4 C sugar
1/4 tbs cinnamon   1/4 tsp salt
1 tbs plus 1 tsp baking powder   1/2 C oil
2 eggs, beaten

Combine dry ingredients; add oil and eggs, blend.
Add nuts and berries, blend to moisten. Fill 12
greased tins 3/4 full; bake at 400o 20-25 minutes.

STRAWBERRY BLUEBERRY BANANA

1 egg, beaten
1/4 C vegetable oil
1/4 C sugar
1/2 tsp salt
1/2 C strawberries

1/2 C milk
2 C flour
3 tsp baking powder
1/4 C mashed banana
1/2 C blueberries

Combine egg, milk and oil; stir in wet ingredients,
mix to a lumpy batter; fold in berries. Fill 12
greased tins 3/4 full; bake at 400o 20-25 minutes.

STREUSEL SURPRISE

1½ C flour
1¼ tsp baking powder
1/8 tsp ginger
1/4 tsp salt
1 egg, beaten

1/4 C sugar
1/2 tsp cinnamon
1/4 tsp baking soda
1/4 C margarine, soft
1/2 C buttermilk

* * *

Streusel topping: 3 tbs flour, 3 tbs brown sugar,
1/2 tsp cinnamon, 2 tbs margarine (soft), 4 tbs
chopped nuts. Combine flour, sugar, cinnamon; cut
in margarine until mixture is crumbly; add nuts.
Set aside for awhile.
In another bowl, mix dry ingredients; cut in
margarine until mixture is crumbly. In small bowl,
combine egg and buttermilk; add to dry mixture;

stir to lumpy batter. Spoon 1/2 batter into 12
greased tins, filling each 1/3 full. Top with
with half the topping, remaining batter, and
remaining topping; 400o for 15-20 minutes.

SUNNYSIDE

1 C whole wheat flour
1 tsp baking soda
1/4 tsp nutmeg
1/4 C sunflower seeds
1/2 C coconut
2 eggs, beaten
1 tsp vanilla extract

1/3 C sugar
1/2 tsp cinnamon
1½ C shredded carrot
1/3 C chocolate chips
1 banana, mashed
1/2 C vegetable oil

Combine flour, sugar, soda, spices; mix. Stir in carrot, seeds, chips, coconut, banana. In another bowl, beat egg, oil, vanilla; add to dry items, moisten. Fill 12 greased tins 2/3 full; bake at 375o for 18-20 minutes.

SWEET POTATO

1 3/4 C flour	1/4 C sugar
1 tbs baking powder	1 tbs brown sugar
1/2 tsp salt	1/2 C chopped nuts
1¼ C cooked and mashed sweet potatoes	
3/4 C milk	2 eggs, beaten
1/2 C margarine, melted	1/4 C sugar
1/4 tsp nutmeg	1/2 tsp cinnamon

Combine first six ingredients in large bowl, make

a well in center. In another bowl, combine next
four ingredients, pour into well, moisten. Fill 12
greased tins 2/3 full. Combine sugar and spices,
sprinkle over each muffin; 425o for 20-25 minutes.
Variation: **SWEET POTATO—APPLE** - Substitute 1/2 C
chopped apple for nuts in the Sweet Potato recipe.

VANILLA
(SUGAR-FREE)

1 egg, beaten
1 4½ serving package sugar-free vanilla pudding
2 C flour
1/2 tsp salt
1/2 tsp cinnamon

1 3/4-2 C milk
3 tsp baking powder
1/4 tsp nutmeg
2 tsp vanilla

Combine egg, milk, oil and pudding. Stir in other
ingredients; mix well. Fill 12 greased tins 3/4 full;
bake at 400o for 20-25 minutes.

WHOLE WHEAT

1/2 C margarine, melted
1 egg, beaten
1/4 tsp salt
1 tsp baking soda

1 C brown sugar
1 C milk
2 C whole wheat flour
1/4 tsp nutmeg (opt)

Combine margarine and brown sugar, add eggs. Mix
dry ingredients in another bowl; combine mixtures,
blend well. Fill 12 greased tins 2/3 full; bake at
400o for 20 minutes.
Variation: **WHOLE WHEAT-BLUEBERRY** - Add 1/2 C
blueberries (if frozen, thaw and pat dry) to the
Whole Wheat recipe.

ZUCCHINI

2 eggs, beaten
1/2 C honey
1/2 C margarine, melted
1 tsp baking soda
1/2 tsp baking powder
1/4 tsp nutmeg
3/4 C chopped nuts
2 C shredded zucchini

1/2 C brown sugar
1 tsp vanilla extract
1 3/4 C flour
1/2 tsp salt
1/2 tsp cinnamon
1 C rolled oats
1/2 C raisins (opt)

In large bowl, beat into eggs sugar, honey, vanilla, margarine. In another bowl, mix flour, baking soda, salt, baking powder, spices; add to egg mixture, stir until moist. Stir in oats, nuts, raisins and zucchini. Fill 12-15 greased tins 3/4 full; bake at 350o for 25 minutes (until toothpick is clean).

ZUCCHINI CARROT

1 egg, beaten
1/2 C vegetable oil
1/4 C sugar
1/2 tsp salt
1/4 tsp allspice
1/2 C zucchini, shredded

3/4 C milk
2 C flour
3 tsp baking powder
1/2 tsp cinnamon

1/2 C carrot, shredded

Combine egg, milk, oil; stir in remaining ingredients and mix into a lumpy batter. Fill 12 greased tins 3/4 full; bake at 400o for 20-25 minutes.
Variation: **ZUCCHINI PINEAPPLE** - Substitute 4 oz crushed pineapple (drained) for the carrot in the above recipe.

NEED GIFTS?

Are you up a stump for some nice gifts for some nice people in your life? Here's a list of some great cookbooks. Just check 'em off, stick a check in an envelope with this page, and we'll get your books off to you. Add $2.75 for shipping and handling for the first book and then $.50 cents more for each additional one. If you order over $50.00, forget the shipping and handling.

Mini Cookbooks
(Only 3 1/2 x 5) With Maxi Good Eatin' - 160 or 176 pages - $5.95

- ☐ Arizona Cooking
- ☐ Arkansas Cooking
- ☐ Dakota Cooking
- ☐ Illinois Cooking
- ☐ Indiana Cooking
- ☐ Iowa Cookin'
- ☐ Kansas Cookin'
- ☐ Kentucky Cooking
- ☐ Michigan Cooking
- ☐ Minnesota Cookin'
- ☐ Missouri Cookin'
- ☐ New Jersey Cooking
- ☐ New Mexico Cooking
- ☐ New York Cooking
- ☐ Ohio Cooking
- ☐ Pennsylvania Cooking
- ☐ Wisconsin Cooking
- ☐ Amish Mennonite Apple Cookbook
- ☐ Amish Mennonite Berry Cookbook
- ☐ Amish Mennonite Peach Cookbook
- ☐ Amish Mennonite Pumpkin Cookbook
- ☐ Amish & Mennonite Strawberry Cookbook
- ☐ Apples! Apples! Apples!
- ☐ Apples Galore
- ☐ Basil A-Z
- ☐ Berries! Berries! Berries!
- ☐ Berries Galore!
- ☐ Bountiful Blueberries

- ☐ Cherries! Cherries! Cherries!
- ☐ Cherries Galore
- ☐ Citrus! Citrus! Citrus!
- ☐ Cooking Beef, Pork & Lamb with Wine
- ☐ Cooking Seafood & Poultry with Wine
- ☐ Cooking with Asparagus
- ☐ Cooking with Cider
- ☐ Cooking with Fresh Basil
- ☐ Cooking with Fresh Herbs
- ☐ Cooking with Garlic
- ☐ Cooking with Spirits
- ☐ Cooking with Sweet Onions
- ☐ Cooking with Wine
- ☐ Cooking with Things Go Baa
- ☐ Cooking with Things Go Cluck
- ☐ Cooking with Things Go Moo
- ☐ Cooking with Things Go Oink
- ☐ Cooking with Things Go Splash
- ☐ Crazy for Basil
- ☐ Crockpot Cookbook
- ☐ Good Cookin' From the Plain People
- ☐ How to Make Salsa
- ☐ Kid Cookin'
- ☐ Kid Fun
- ☐ Kid Money
- ☐ Kid Pumpkin Fun Book
- ☐ Midwest Small Town Cookin'
- ☐ Muffins Cookbook (Veggies, Fruit, Nut)

- ☐ Nuts! Nuts! Nuts!
- ☐ Off To College Cookbook
- ☐ Peaches! Peaches! Peaches!
- ☐ Pecans! Pecans! Pecans!
- ☐ Pumpkins! Pumpkins! Pumpkins!
- ☐ Recipes for Appetizers & Beverages Using Wine
- ☐ Recipes for Desserts Using Wine
- ☐ Some Like It Hot
- ☐ Soup's On!
- ☐ Southwest Cooking
- ☐ Squash Cookbook
- ☐ Super Simple Cookin'
- ☐ To Take the *Gamey* out of the Game Cookbook
- ☐ Working Girl Cookbook

Larger Mini Cookbooks
176 - 204 pages - $6.95
- ☐ Cooking with Mulling Spices
- ☐ Grass-Fed Beef Recipes
- ☐ Holiday & Get-Together Cookbook
- ☐ Veggie Talk Coloring & Story Book

In-Between Cookbooks
(5 1/2 x 8 1/2) - 150 pages - $9.95
- ☐ Adaptable Apple Cookbook
- ☐ Amish Ladies Cookbook - Old Husbands
- ☐ Amish Ladies Cookbook - Young Husbands
- ☐ Baseball Moms' Cookbook
- ☐ Basketball Moms' Cookbook
- ☐ Bird Up! Pheasant Cookbook
- ☐ Buffalo Cookbook

HEARTS 'N TUMMIES COOKBOOK CO.
3544 Blakslee St. • Wever, Iowa 52658
1-800-571-2665

Name _____

Address _____

_____ Ph.# _____

*You Iowa folks gotta kick in another 6% for Sales Tax.